The Understanding Your Suicide Grief
Journal

D1113509

Also by Alan Wolfelt

The Handbook for Companioning the Mourner:
Eleven Essential Principles

Healing Your Traumatized Heart:100 Practical Ideas After
Someone You Love Dies a Sudden, Violent Death

The Journey Through Grief:
Reflections on Healing

Understanding Your Suicide Grief: Ten Essential Touchstones for
Finding Hope and Healing Your Heart

The Understanding Your Suicide Grief Support Group Guide:
Meeting Plans for Facilitators

The Wilderness of Suicide Grief:
Finding Your Way

Companion
P R E S S

Companion Press is dedicated to the education and support of both the bereaved and bereavement caregivers. We believe that those who companion the bereaved by walking with them as they journey in grief have a wondrous opportunity: to help others embrace and grow through grief—and to lead fuller, more deeply-lived lives themselves because of this important ministry.

For a complete catalog and ordering information, write or call:

Companion Press
The Center for Loss and Life Transition
3735 Broken Bow Road
Fort Collins, Colorado 80526
(970) 226-6050

www.centerforloss.com

The Understanding Your Suicide Grief Journal

A companion workbook to the book
Understanding Your Suicide Grief

Alan D. Wolfelt, Ph.D.

Companion
PRESS

Fort Collins, Colorado
An imprint of the Center for Loss and Life Transition

Companion Press is an imprint of the Center for Loss and Life Transition, 3735 Broken Bow Road, Fort Collins, Colorado 80526.

Printed in the United States of America.

17 16 15 14 13 12 11 10 09   5 4 3 2 1

ISBN: 978-1-879651-59-3

Contents

Introduction

"Writing is the most profound way of codifying your thoughts, the best way of learning from yourself who you are and what you believe."

Warren Bennis

I have written this journal as a companion to my book *Understanding Your Suicide Grief: Ten Essential Touchstones for Finding Hope and Healing Your Heart.* My hope is that this guided journal can be a "safe place" for you to explore your experience with the ten essential Touchstones.

As you tell your story, your words will guide you on your unique journey through the wilderness of your grief. Your words will also give testimony to the love you will always have for the person who has died. You can use the journal not only to understand your grief, but to remember, celebrate, and commemorate the life of the person to whom you dedicate this journal.

The Value of Journaling

Journaling has proven to be an excellent way for many people to do the work of mourning. Journaling is private and independent, yet it's still expressing your grief outside of yourself. I've been a grief counselor for a long time now (over 30 years!), and I've found that while it may not be for everyone, the process of putting the written word on paper is profoundly helpful to many grieving people in the following ways:

Journaling...

• honors the person who died by suicide.

• clarifies what you're thinking and feeling.

• creates a safe place of solace, a place where you can fully express yourself no matter what you are experiencing.

• allows you to tap into the Touchstones of the companion book.

• helps soften the intensity of your thoughts and feelings and helps you better understand both your grief and your mourning.

• clears out your naturally overwhelmed mind and full heart.

• examines the pain you are experiencing and transforms it into something survivable.

• creates an opportunity to acknowledge the balance in your life between the sad and the happy.

• strengthens your awareness of how your grief journey changes over time.

• maps out your transformation as you journey through grief.

As one author observed, "When you write, you lay out a line of words. The line of words is a miner's pick, a woodcarver's gouge, a surgeon's probe. You wield it, and it digs a path you follow." To this I would add that a grief journal can provide a lifeline when you are in the midst of the wilderness. As you learn, remember, and discover new things, you can and will integrate this grief into your life and go on to find meaning and purpose in your continued life's journey.

Journaling Suggestions

First, please remember that there is no "correct" or "right" way to use this journal. You will not be graded on how quickly you complete the pages that follow. Actually, I would suggest that you take your time. If you are using this resource as part of a support group experience, your leaders will probably "dose" the completing of this journal over weeks or months.

If you are reading *Understanding Your Suicide Grief* and completing this journal on your own, I suggest you find a trusted person who can be available to you if and when you want to talk out any thoughts and feelings the journal brings up for you. When I say a trusted person, I mean someone who accepts you where you are right now in your grief journey. This person shouldn't judge you or think it's his or her job to "get you over" your grief quickly. Remember—there are no rewards for speed!

You will notice that in addition to the guided journal sections, in which you are asked to answer specific questions about your unique grief journey, there are a number of "Free Write" pages. These are places for you to freely write about whatever is on your heart as you are completing the journal. At the end of the journal, you will also find a section entitled "Continuing Your Journey." This is a place to write down your ongoing thoughts and feelings about this profound loss in the years to come.

- **Setting**
  Pick a safe place to write in your journal. Naturally, journaling is usually easier to do in a quiet place that is free from interruptions and distractions.

- **Honesty**
  If an effort to open yourself to your grief and mourning, you must be honest with yourself. You must think your true thoughts and write them out, feel your true feelings and express them.

- Privacy
  This is your journal and yours alone. Remember—you don't have to share your journal or show it to anyone you don't want to. If you are participating in a support group, you may be invited to share some of what you write in your journal. Yet, keep in mind that sharing should always be optional, not mandatory.

Be Gentle with Yourself

Some people shy away from writing in a journal because they don't think they are good writers. It doesn't matter if you're a "good writer" or not, at least in the English teacher sense of that term. The point isn't to test your vocabulary or your punctuation or even your creative writing skills, but to explore what is on your mind and in your heart. Don't criticize what you find comes to paper. Ignore your penmanship and don't worry about grammar or spelling. This journal is for you. Journaling is a breathing space on paper. Breathe deep and go forth!

Remember to be Kind to Yourself

A journal is a confessor. It simply listens as you write. Believe in your ability to set your intention to heal by using the journal as one instrument in your healing. Remember to be kind to yourself during this naturally difficult journey.

Sincerely,

Alan D. Wolfelt

DEDICATION

I dedicate this journal in memory of

_____
(name of the person who died)

Your name

_____

Your relationship to the person who died

_____

Place a photograph below of your special person who has died:

This photo is special to me because

_____
_____
_____

Welcome

An Invitation to Open Your Heart

*"Surrounded by my memories, I took
my pen and began to write."*
Kuki Gallmann

This guided journal is a safe place for you to express your many
thoughts, feelings, and memories. The purpose of this kind of
guided journal is, in part, to help you learn to understand your
grief and become friends with it. This resource is intended to
help you open your heart and explore how someone's death has
changed your life. My hope is that this journal will help you in
your healing and honor your relationship with someone who has
been a special part of your life here on planet Earth.

I urge you not to skip over reading the section titled, "Welcome: An Invitation to Open Your Heart." Please take some time to read this section (pp. 5 to 20) and use the following space to reflect on any thoughts that come to mind in the following space:

_____

_____

_____

_____

_____

_____

_____

_____

_____

_____

_____

_____

_____

_____

_____

_____

_____

_____

_____

_____

_____

_____

_____

_____

Touchstone One

Open to the Presence of Your Loss

In the companion text…

We discussed the necessity of opening to the presence of your loss. To heal in grief, you must honor—not avoid—the pain. One way to embrace the pain while at the same time maintaining hope for the future is by setting your intention to heal. Even as you embrace your pain and set your intention to heal, remember that healing in grief does not happen quickly or efficiently. Also remember that the common perception of "doing well" in grief is erroneous. To "do well" with your grief, you must not be strong and silent, but rather mourn openly and honestly.

As you were reading *Understanding Your Suicide Grief*, you discovered that honoring your grief means "recognizing the value of" and "respecting" your grief. You learned that while it is not instinctive to view the grief that follows a death to suicide as something you want to honor, this death requires that you mourn. You also learned that it is not self-destructive or harmful. It is self-sustaining and life-giving!

HONORING YOUR GRIEF

Describe any ways in which you have honored your grief. If you feel you have not been honoring your grief, write about ways you could be doing so.

_____

_____

_____

_____

_____

_____

_____

_____

DOSING YOUR PAIN

The pain of your grief will keep trying to get your attention until you have the courage to gently, and in small doses, embrace it. How is the pain of your grief trying to get your attention? (See p. 27 of *Understanding Your Suicide Grief* for a definition of dosing your pain.)

_____

_____

_____

_____

_____

_____

SOUL WORK AND SPIRIT WORK

You have learned that there is an important distinction between "soul work" and "spirit work." In addition, you now realize that "soul work" precedes "spirit work" on the path to integrating this loss into your life. Where do you see yourself right now in this process that you are now aware you must experience?

_____

_____

_____

_____

_____

_____

_____

_____

_____

SETTING YOUR INTENTION TO HEAL

When you set your intention to heal, you make a true commitment to positively influence the course of your journey. You choose between being what I would call a "passive witness" to your grief or an "active participant" in your grief. Describe below your understanding of the difference between being a "passive witness" to your grief or an "active participant" in your grief:

_____

_____

_____

_____

_____

_____

_____

_____

INTEGRATING YOUR SUICIDE GRIEF

You learned that when you set your intention to heal, you make a true commitment to positively influence the course of your journey. Use the space below to explore your intention to heal in grief.

_____

_____

_____

_____

_____

_____

_____

_____

_____

_____

_____

_____

_____

_____

_____

_____

_____

_____

_____

_____

_____

_____

_____

NO REWARD FOR SPEED

Reconciling your grief does not happen quickly or efficiently. How do you feel about your capacity to go slow and be patient with yourself in your journey through grief?

_____

_____

_____

_____

_____

_____

_____

_____

_____

_____

_____

_____

_____

_____

_____

_____

_____

_____

_____

_____

_____

_____

_____

_____

_____

_____

SHOCK VERSUS DENIAL

You learned there is a real difference between shock and long-term denial. You learned there are different sub-types of denial. Explore any thoughts you have related to this topic.

FACE ANY INAPPROPRIATE EXPECTATIONS

Sometimes people who are openly mourning feel ashamed of their thoughts, feelings, and behaviors. Do you feel any sense of shame or embarrassment about how your grief feels or how you are mourning? If so, write about it below.

_____

_____

_____

_____

_____

_____

_____

_____

GRIEF IS NOT A DISEASE

While grief is a powerful experience, so, too, is your ability to help in your own healing.

Write about any steps you've taken (even baby steps!) to help yourself begin to heal.

_____

_____

_____

_____

_____

_____

_____

_____

_____

_____

15

Touchstone Two

Dispel the Misconceptions About Suicide and Grief and Mourning

In the companion text…

We discovered that many of the perceptions we may have had—and society often teaches us—about suicide and grief and mourning aren't true at all. For example, grief does NOT progress in predictable, orderly stages. And tears aren't a sign of weakness; actually, they're a form of mourning and they are natural and necessary. Many misconceptions color our expectations about grief. The trick is to sort out the fact from the fiction and grieve and mourn in healthy, authentic ways.

MISCONCEPTION 1: Grief and mourning are the same thing.

Did you used to think that grief and mourning were the same thing? If so, how has this misconception affected you?

_____

_____

_____

_____

_____

Now that we've explored the difference between grief and mourning, how will you mourn this death—that is, openly and honestly express your grief outside of yourself?

_____

_____

_____

_____

_____

Do you see yourself having difficulty with expressing your grief outside of yourself (mourning) in any ways? If so, what ways?

_____

_____

_____

_____

_____

_____

_____

MISCONCEPTION 2: Grief following a suicide death always results in "complicated" or "pathological" mourning.

You have learned that while a suicide death may be viewed differently because of the circumstances, research indicates that survivors integrate the grief at about the same pace as those who experience any kind of unanticipated death. How do you feel about that?

_____

_____

_____

_____

_____

Have you heard about the "stages of grief"? If so, what is or was your feeling about this popular grief model?

_____

_____

_____

Since the "stages of grief" model isn't really accurate, how do you believe you will move forward in your own unique journey through grief?

_____

_____

_____

Grief is often a one step forward, two steps back process. How could you help yourself during those inevitable times when you think you're moving backwards instead of forwards?

_____

_____

_____

MISCONCEPTION 3: Grief and mourning progress in predictable, orderly stages.

Have you felt pressured to "overcome" your grief instead of experiencing it? If so, how and why have you been pressured?

_____

_____

_____

_____

_____

_____

_____

What does it mean to you to move toward your pain?

_____

_____

_____

_____

_____

How could you deal with friends, family, coworkers, etc. who encourage you (either outright or implicitly) to move away from your grief?

_____

_____

_____

_____

_____

_____

_____

MISCONCEPTION 4: We can always determine the "whys?" of suicide death.

Write about the thoughts and feelings you have had about why this person took his or her own life.

_____

_____

_____

_____

_____

_____

_____

_____

_____

_____

_____

_____

Do you believe you may never fully understand why? If so, how do you feel about living with this uncertainty?

_____

_____

_____

_____

_____

_____

_____

_____

_____

_____

_____

_____

MISCONCEPTION 5: All suicide survivors feel guilty.

You have learned that guilt is one of the most prescribed responses for a survivor of suicide. Yet, you were reminded you may or may not feel guilty.

Have you had anyone prescribe to you that you should feel guilty or asked you if you do? If so, what has this been like for you?

_____

_____

_____

_____

_____

_____

_____

_____

_____

_____

Do you, or do you not, have any feeling of guilt? If so, write about your guilt here.

_____

_____

_____

_____

_____

_____

_____

_____

MISCONCEPTION 6: Only certain kinds of people complete suicide.

Have you been told that only certain "kinds" of people complete suicide? If so, what have you been told? What do you now understand related to this misconception?

_____

_____

_____

_____

_____

_____

_____

_____

_____

MISCONCEPTION 7: Only a crazy person completes suicide.

Has anyone told you the person who completed suicide was "crazy"? If so, how does this make you feel? What can you say to help people understand that while these comments may be well-intended, this doesn't bring you comfort?

_____

_____

_____

_____

_____

_____

_____

_____

MISCONCEPTION 8: It is a sin to complete suicide, and the person who does goes straight to hell.

What are your thoughts related to suicide and sin? Were you taught anything about this when you were growing up, and, if so, what? Where are you with this now?

_____

_____

_____

_____

_____

_____

_____

_____

_____

_____

_____

MISCONCEPTION 9: Suicide is inherited and runs in the family.

Has anyone told you that suicide is inherited? If so, describe below. What do you now understand about this misconception?

_____

_____

_____

_____

_____

_____

_____

_____

MISCONCEPTION 10: You should move away from suicide grief, not toward it.

You have learned that society often encourages you to move away from your suicide grief. Some people would like you to be "back to normal" quickly and efficiently. Use the space below to write about what you have learned about the need to move toward your grief, not away from your grief.

_____

_____

_____

_____

_____

_____

_____

_____

MISCONCEPTION 11: Tears of grief are only a sign of weakness.

What has your experience with tears been since the death?

_____

_____

_____

_____

_____

_____

_____

_____

_____

_____

Do others around you make you feel any sense of shame or weakness about crying? If so, who and why?

_____

_____

_____

_____

_____

_____

_____

_____

_____

_____

_____

MISCONCEPTION 12: Being upset and openly mourning means you are being weak in your faith.

Are you a person of faith or consider yourself to be a spiritual person? Do you believe in God or a power greater than yourself? Use the space below to write about your personal beliefs.

_____

_____

_____

_____

_____

_____

_____

_____

_____

Do you think you are being weak in your faith/spiritual life if you are struggling with this death? Or has anyone else made you feel this way? What is your understanding of the relationship between "having faith" and needing to openly mourn?

_____

_____

_____

_____

_____

_____

_____

_____

MISCONCEPTION 13: When someone you love completes suicide, you only grieve and mourn for the physical loss of the person.

You have come to realize that when someone completes suicide, you don't just lose the presence of the person. List some of the "secondary losses" you are experiencing as a result of this death.

_____

_____

_____

_____

_____

_____

_____

_____

From the list above, choose one or two of your most significant secondary losses and write about them here.

_____

_____

_____

_____

_____

_____

_____

_____

_____

_____

MISCONCEPTION 14: You should try not to think about the person who completed suicide on holidays, anniversaries, and birthdays.

Since the death, have you encountered a holiday, anniversary date, or birthday that was connected to the person who died? Describe what you did on this day and how you felt.

_____

_____

_____

_____

_____

_____

_____

_____

_____

_____

_____

On this day, did you try to avoid thinking about the person who died or did you try to honor your grief and the memory of the person who died? Write about your choice and how it turned out for you.

_____

_____

_____

_____

_____

_____

_____

_____

_____

_____

What is the next upcoming holiday, anniversary, or birthday connected to the person who died? How could you commemorate the life of the person who died on this day?

_____

_____

_____

_____

_____

_____

_____

_____

_____

_____

_____

MISCONCEPTION 15: After someone you love completes suicide, you should be able to "get over" grief as soon as possible.

What thoughts do you have when you hear people talk about "getting over" grief?

_____

_____

_____

_____

_____

_____

_____

Has anyone else told you or made you feel that you need to "get over" your grief? If so, who and in what circumstances? How did this make you feel?

_____

_____

_____

_____

_____

_____

_____

How do you feel about the reality that you do not get over your grief but rather learn to reconcile yourself to it?

_____

_____

_____

_____

_____

MISCONCEPTION 16: Nobody can help you with your grief.

Are you normally an independent person who does everything for him/herself, or are you an interdependent person who relies on others for help with some things? Explain.

_____

_____

_____

_____

_____

_____

In order to heal, you will need to reach out to others to help you with your grief. Do you believe this to be true? Why or why not?

_____

_____

_____

_____

_____

List at least three people who would be (or are) naturally good companions for you on your journey though the wilderness of your grief.

_____

_____

_____

_____

_____

MISCONCEPTION 17: When grief and mourning are finally reconciled, they never come up again.

This misconception is a close cousin to Misconception 14, which says that your goal should be to "get over" your grief as soon as possible. Grief doesn't end, but it does erupt less frequently. Have you had any recent "eruptions" you could write about?

_____

_____

_____

_____

_____

_____

_____

_____

Do you have any "grief role models" in your life—people who mourned openly and honestly after a death and went on to reconcile their grief and continue to live a life of meaning and joy? If so, who? How does this person (or these people) continue to acknowledge and honor his or her grief in the years and decades after the death?

_____

_____

_____

_____

_____

_____

_____

_____

_____

Touchstone Three

Explore the Uniqueness of Your Suicide Grief

In the companion text...

We developed an understanding that each person's grief is unique and that grief and mourning can never be strictly compared. We also explored all the many reasons that your grief is *your* grief—why it is unique to you and unlike anyone else's.

WHY #1 The Circumstances of the Suicide

A number of specific features surrounding potential aspects of your experience were outlined in this section. Take a moment to re-read the features described here. Now, use the space below to write about the ones that have application to your experience. Add any additional circumstances that apply to you.

_____

_____

_____

_____

_____

_____

_____

_____

_____

_____

WHY #2 Your Relationship with the Person Who Completed Suicide

If someone asked you to describe your relationship with the person who died, what would immediately come to your head and your heart?

_____

_____

_____

_____

_____

_____

_____

_____

How attached were you to this person?

_____

_____

_____

_____

_____

_____

_____

_____

_____

_____

_____

Describe how you acted and felt in one another's company.

_____

_____

_____

_____

_____

_____

_____

_____

_____

_____

_____

Can you remember a time when you felt very close to this person? Please describe it here.

_____

_____

_____

_____

_____

_____

_____

_____

_____

_____

_____

Were there times when it was difficult to get along with this person? If so, give some examples of those times. If not, write about why you think you got along so well.

_____

_____

_____

_____

_____

_____

_____

_____

_____

_____

What did the person who died look like?

Approximate height_____   Approximate weight_____

Hair color_____   Eye color_____

Other distinguishing characteristics:

_____

_____

_____

_____

_____

_____

_____

_____

Write about two special memories you will always have of your relationship with the person who died.

_____

_____

_____

_____

_____

_____

_____

_____

_____

_____

_____

_____

_____

_____

WHY #3 The People in Your Life

Do you have people in your life (friends and family) whom you can turn to for help and support? List them.

_____

_____

_____

_____

_____

What qualities do these people have that make them able to "walk with" you in your grief?

_____

_____

_____

_____

_____

Are there people in your life you could turn to for support but for some reason you don't feel you can? If so, who and why?

_____

_____

_____

_____

_____

Are you willing to accept support from friends and family? If not, why not?

_____

_____

_____

_____

_____

Sometimes well-meaning friends and family will hurt you unknowingly with their words. They may tell you:

- "I know how you feel." (They don't.)
- "Get on with your life." (You're not ready to.)
- "Keep your chin up." (You have every right to be sad.)
- "Time heals all wounds." (Time helps, but it alone doesn't heal.)
- "He/she wouldn't want you to be sad." (Maybe not, but he/she would also understand why you are!)

Have you had anyone say things like this to you? If so, write out an example and describe how it made you feel.

_____

_____

_____

_____

What are some things that people have said or done that have been helpful to you?

_____

_____

_____

_____

Do you have friends at work, at your place of worship, and/or at an organization you are a part of who are supportive of your grief? Who are these people, and how can you continue to reach out to them?

_____

_____

_____

_____

Are you attending a support group as you work through this journal and companion text? If so, can you describe how this group experience is going for you so far?

_____

_____

_____

_____

_____

_____

_____

_____

_____

_____

Are you seeing a counselor who is helping you work through this journal and companion text? If so, what has the counseling experience been like for you so far?

_____

_____

_____

_____

_____

_____

_____

_____

_____

_____

_____

_____

WHY #4 Your Unique Personality

What are some adjectives you would use to describe yourself?

_____

_____

_____

_____

_____

How do you think your unique personality is influencing your grief and mourning?

_____

_____

_____

_____

_____

Of the three personality types described in this section (thinker, feeler, stoic), which one is more likely to describe you and why?

_____

_____

_____

_____

_____

How have you responded to other life losses or crises in your life?

_____

_____

_____

_____

Are you responding in a similar way now, or does this loss feel different? Explain.

_____

_____

_____

_____

_____

Do you think your personality has changed as a result of this death? If so, how? If not, why not?

_____

_____

_____

_____

How is your self-esteem right now?

_____

_____

_____

_____

Do you think this death has impacted how you feel about yourself? If so, how?

_____

_____

_____

_____

WHY #5 The Unique Personality of the Person Who Completed Suicide

Check off the following personality traits that seem to describe the person who died.

___ accepting	___ active	___ adventuresome
___ aggressive	___ annoying	___ anxious
___ argumentative	___ artistic	___ big-hearted
___ calm	___ caring	___ charming
___ clever	___ cold	___ compassionate
___ competitive	___ conceited	___ confident
___ controlling	___ cooperative	___ courageous
___ creative	___ critical	___ demanding
___ dependable	___ detached	___ direct
___ dramatic	___ dynamic	___ emotional
___ energetic	___ enthusiastic	___ fair
___ forgetful	___ friendly	___ funny
___ good-natured	___ graceful	___ honest
___ hyperactive	___ imaginative	___ independent
___ inflexible	___ influential	___ insecure
___ interesting	___ inventive	___ irritable
___ jealous	___ logical	___ loud
___ moody	___ nervous	___ nurturing
___ opinionated	___ outgoing	___ overprotective
___ overwhelming	___ perfectionistic	___ persuasive
___ playful	___ protective	___ punctual
___ quick to anger	___ rebellious	___ resourceful
___ rude	___ romantic	___ scatterbrained
___ self-centered	___ sensitive	___ shy
___ sincere	___ smart	___ spiritual
___ spontaneous	___ stubborn	___ temperamental
___ tireless	___ troubled	___ trustworthy
___ two-faced	___ warm	___ wise
___ witty	___ wonderful	___ worried

Now, in your own words, describe the personality of the person who died.

_____

_____

_____

_____

_____

_____

_____

_____

_____

_____

_____

_____

_____

_____

_____

_____

_____

_____

_____

_____

_____

_____

_____

_____

Place a photo of the person who died here, one that you think expresses his or her unique personality.

What roles did this person play in your life? (For example, husband, best friend, advisor, lover, anchor, etc.)

_____

_____

_____

_____

_____

_____

How did this person's unique personality affect the roles he or she played in your life?

_____

_____

_____

_____

_____

_____

_____

What personality traits of this person did you enjoy the most?

_____

_____

_____

_____

_____

_____

_____

_____

Give an example of a time when these personality traits really shone through in this person.

_____

_____

_____

_____

_____

_____

_____

_____

_____

_____

_____

_____

_____

_____

What personality traits of this person did you least enjoy?

_____

_____

_____

_____

_____

_____

_____

_____

_____

_____

_____

Give an example of a time when these negative traits were apparent to you.

_____

_____

_____

_____

_____

_____

_____

_____

_____

_____

_____

_____

_____

_____

_____

_____

_____

_____

_____

If you were asked to list the three personality traits you admired the most in this person, what would those be? (You might want to review the checklist on p. 43.)

_____

_____

_____

WHY #6 Your Gender

Do you think that being a man or a woman affects your grief? If so, how? If not, why not?

_____

_____

_____

_____

_____

_____

_____

_____

Has your gender influenced how people support you in your grief? If so, how?

_____

_____

_____

_____

_____

_____

_____

In grief, do you see any advantages or disadvantages to being the gender you are?

_____

_____

_____

_____

_____

WHY #7 Your Cultural/Ethnic/Religious/Spiritual Background

What is your cultural background?

_____

_____

_____

_____

_____

_____

_____

_____

How does this background influence your grief and mourning?

_____

_____

_____

_____

_____

_____

_____

If you were asked to articulate them, what would you say some of your family's "rules" were about coping with loss and grief? In what ways did you see these rules carried out?

_____

_____

_____

_____

_____

_____

How do you feel about these rules and their helpfulness to you
(or unhelpfulness to you) in grief?

_____

_____

_____

_____

_____

_____

_____

Did you grow up with certain religious or spiritual teachings?
Please describe them.

_____

_____

_____

_____

_____

Have your religious or spiritual beliefs changed over time? If so,
describe how they have changed.

_____

_____

_____

_____

_____

_____

_____

_____

How has death affected your belief system? Be specific.

_____

_____

_____

_____

_____

_____

_____

_____

_____

Do you have people around you who understand and support you in your belief system? If so, who are these people and how can they help you now?

_____

_____

_____

_____

_____

_____

_____

_____

Do you think that your faith, religion, or spiritual background is playing a part in your healing process? Please explain.

_____

_____

_____

_____

_____

_____

WHY #8 Other Crises or Stresses in Your Life Right Now

What other losses have come about in your life either as a result of the death or coincidentally during the same time frame?

_____

_____

_____

_____

How do you see these other losses influencing your grief?

_____

_____

_____

_____

What other stresses or crises are a part of your life right now?

_____

_____

_____

_____

How are they affecting your grief?

_____

_____

_____

_____

Whom can you turn to right now to help you cope with these secondary losses or stresses?

_____

_____

_____

WHY #9 Your Experience with Loss and Death in the Past

Have you had other significant death losses in your life? If so, please describe them.

_____

_____

_____

_____

_____

_____

_____

Compared to these previous grief journeys, how does this grief journey feel for you and why?

_____

_____

_____

_____

_____

_____

_____

Have you experienced any significant non-death losses in your life, such as divorce, job loss, etc? If so, write them down and consider how they might now be affecting your grief.

_____

_____

_____

_____

_____

_____

_____

WHY #10 Your Physical Health

You'll be writing more about this on p. 112 of this journal.
For now, take a moment to write about how you are feeling
physically right now.

_____

_____

_____

_____

_____

_____

_____

_____

_____

_____

_____

_____

_____

_____

_____

OTHER WHYS

Are there other factors, large or small, that are influencing your
grief right now? If so, write about them here.

_____

_____

_____

_____

_____

_____

_____

_____

Free Write

_____
_____
_____
_____
_____
_____
_____
_____
_____
_____
_____
_____
_____
_____
_____
_____
_____
_____
_____
_____
_____
_____
_____
_____
_____
_____
_____
_____
_____
_____
_____

Touchstone Four

Exploring Your Feelings of Loss

In this chapter in the companion text...

We agreed that as strange as your emotions may seem, they are a true expression of where you are right now in your journey through grief. We emphasized that whatever your grief thoughts and feelings are, they are normal and necessary. Feelings aren't right or wrong, they just are. Naming the feelings and acknowledging them are the first steps to integrating them into your life. It's actually the process of becoming friendly with your feelings that will help you heal.

Before exploring some of your possible responses to the death of your special person, please take a moment to write out a few words that describe how you are feeling right now. In the space below, complete the following statement:

Right now, I'm feeling...

_____

_____

_____

_____

_____

_____

_____

_____

_____

_____

SHOCK, NUMBNESS, DENIAL, AND DISBELIEF

Have you felt "in shock" or "numb" since the death? What was this like for you?

_____

_____

_____

_____

_____

_____

_____

_____

_____

_____

_____

Do you feel like your shock and numbness helped you through the early days after the death? If yes, how? If no, why not?

_____

_____

_____

_____

_____

_____

_____

_____

_____

_____

_____

Do you feel that you are or have been in denial about the death? Please explain.

_____

_____

_____

_____

_____

_____

_____

_____

_____

_____

_____

_____

_____

_____

Are you learning to allow yourself to acknowledge the death in small doses in between your periods of denial? In the companion book, I called this EVADE <—> ENCOUNTER. If you are stuck on EVADE, how can you help yourself ENCOUNTER the reality of the death?

_____

_____

_____

_____

_____

_____

_____

How have your feelings of shock, numbness, denial, and disbelief changed or softened since the death?

_____

_____

_____

_____

_____

_____

_____

What are you doing to express your feelings of shock, numbness, denial, and disbelief?

_____

_____

_____

_____

_____

_____

_____

DISORGANIZATION, CONFUSION, SEARCHING, YEARNING

Have you experienced any disorganization and confusion as part of your grieving experience? If so, describe what it has been like for you.

_____

_____

_____

_____

_____

_____

_____

_____

_____

_____

Do you keep starting tasks but never finishing them? Do you forget what you are saying mid-sentence? Are you having trouble getting through your day-to-day commitments? Name some ways in which your grief feelings of disorganization and confusion are affecting your life.

_____

_____

_____

_____

_____

_____

_____

_____

_____

_____

_____

Have you experienced a yearning or searching for the person who died? Please explain.

_____

_____

_____

_____

_____

_____

_____

_____

_____

_____

_____

_____

_____

_____

Do you think you've "seen" or "heard" the person who has died? If so, write about this experience.

_____

_____

_____

_____

_____

_____

_____

_____

_____

_____

_____

Do you dream about the person who died? Describe your dreams.

_____

_____

_____

_____

_____

_____

_____

_____

You learned about "restorative retelling." How does that relate to your experience? Are you retelling your story?

_____

_____

_____

_____

What are you doing to express your feelings of disorganization, confusion, searching, and yearning?

_____

_____

_____

_____

_____

ANXIETY, PANIC, FEAR

Have you felt anxious, fearful, or panicked since the death? If so, please explain.

_____

_____

_____

_____

_____

_____

_____

What are you most afraid of since the death?

_____

_____

_____

_____

_____

_____

_____

What are you doing to express your feelings of anxiety, panic, and fear?

_____

_____

_____

_____

_____

_____

_____

In the space below, write out your ideas and intentions to help yourself with feelings of anxiety, panic, and fear.

_____

_____

_____

_____

_____

_____

_____

_____

_____

_____

_____

_____

_____

_____

_____

_____

_____

_____

_____

_____

_____

_____

_____

_____

_____

_____

_____

_____

_____

_____

_____

_____

_____

_____

EXPLOSIVE EMOTIONS

Have you felt anger, hate, blame, terror, resentment, rage, and/
or jealousy about the death? If not, write about why you think
these feelings haven't been a part of your grief journey so far. If
so, which of these feelings have you experienced? List them here
in the left column then write more about each of your feelings in
the right column.

_____ _____

_____ _____

_____ _____

_____ _____

_____ _____

_____ _____

_____ _____

_____ _____

_____ _____

_____ _____

_____ _____

_____ _____

_____ _____

_____ _____

_____ _____

_____ _____

_____ _____

_____ _____

_____ _____

_____ _____

_____ _____

_____ _____

_____ _____

Have others around you been upset by your expression of these feelings? Explain.

_____

_____

_____

_____

_____

_____

_____

_____

_____

_____

_____

_____

_____

_____

What are you doing to express your explosive emotions in healthy ways?

_____

_____

_____

_____

_____

_____

_____

_____

_____

_____

_____

_____

_____

GUILT, REGRET, SELF-BLAME, SHAME, EMBARRASSMENT

We explored the reality that some people may project any or all of this constellation of experiences onto you. However, we noted that their feelings may or may not be part of your experience.

Have you had any "if onlys" since the death? If so, write about your if-onlys and how they make you feel.

_____

_____

_____

_____

_____

_____

_____

_____

_____

_____

You learned about the relationship between guilt and shame. Is shame a part of your experience? If so, write about it below.

_____

_____

_____

_____

_____

_____

_____

_____

_____

_____

_____

_____

You learned the difference between blame and responsibility.
What thoughts and feelings do you have about this?

_____

_____

_____

_____

_____

_____

_____

_____

_____

_____

_____

_____

_____

Is embarrassment any part of your experience? Write about any
thoughts or experience related to embarrassment below.

_____

_____

_____

_____

_____

_____

_____

_____

_____

_____

_____

_____

Do you think you are experiencing any of the following potential dimensions that were outlined in this section?

___ Relief-guilt

___ Magical thinking and guilt

___ Guilt and means of suicide

___ Parental guilt

___ Spousal guilt

___ Child guilt

___ Mental health caregiver guilt

___ Joy-guilt

___ Longstanding personality factors

I invite you to place checkmarks beside any of the above that fit with your experience and write about them below.

_____

_____

_____

_____

_____

_____

_____

_____

_____

_____

_____

_____

_____

_____

How do other people make you feel about any feelings of guilt, regret, self-blame, shame, or embarrassment?

_____

_____

_____

_____

_____

_____

_____

_____

_____

_____

_____

_____

_____

What are you doing to express any feelings of guilt, regret, self-blame, shame, or embarrassment?

_____

_____

_____

_____

_____

_____

_____

_____

_____

_____

_____

_____

_____

_____

_____

SADNESS, DEPRESSION, LONELINESS, AND VULNERABILITY

Having just read about these feelings, where do you see yourself right now with them?

_____

_____

_____

_____

_____

_____

_____

_____

_____

_____

_____

_____

_____

_____

_____

_____

_____

_____

_____

_____

_____

_____

_____

_____

_____

_____

_____

_____

_____

_____

_____

You learned that sometimes these emotions are experienced in a series or roller coaster cycles, sometimes up, sometimes down. Can you relate to this? If so, write about your personal experience with this below.

_____

_____

_____

_____

_____

_____

_____

_____

_____

_____

_____

_____

To be human is to be vulnerable. What comes to mind when you reflect on the feeling of vulnerability?

_____

_____

_____

_____

_____

_____

_____

_____

_____

_____

_____

_____

_____

You learned that "liminal space" means the space betwixt and between. Can you relate to this? Write about it below.

_____

_____

_____

_____

_____

_____

_____

_____

_____

_____

_____

_____

_____

Has anyone around you tried to subdue or deny your feelings of sadness? If so, write about it below.

_____

_____

_____

_____

_____

_____

_____

_____

_____

_____

_____

_____

_____

_____

_____

_____

If and when you feel sad, depressed, lonely, and/or vulnerable, what can you do to help yourself during these times?

_____

_____

_____

_____

_____

_____

_____

_____

_____

_____

_____

_____

Have you had any thoughts of suicide since the death? If so, please explain.

_____

_____

_____

_____

_____

_____

_____

_____

_____

_____

_____

_____

_____

_____

Keep in mind that transient, passive thoughts of suicide in grief are normal, but persistent, active thoughts of suicide are not.

If you are actively considering or making plans to take your own life, put down this journal this very moment and call someone who will help you get help. If this is an emergency, call 911 immediately.

What are you doing to express your sadness and depression?

CLINICAL DEPRESSION

Do you think you might be clinically depressed instead of just grieving? If yes, review the chart on page 107 in the companion book and determine if you meet any of the criteria for clinical depression. Do you exhibit any of the listed characteristics of clinical depression? If yes, write down your physician's name and phone number in the space below then put down this journal, go to the phone, and make an appointment to see him or her as soon as possible. Remember that getting help for your depression does not mean you are weak; it means you are strong.

Physician's name_____ Phone_____

RELIEF AND RELEASE

Did you feel a sense of relief after the death? If yes, why?

_____

_____

_____

_____

_____

_____

_____

_____

_____

_____

_____

_____

_____

_____

_____

How do you feel about feeling relieved? Do you think it's OK or not OK?

_____

_____

_____

_____

_____

_____

_____

_____

_____

_____

_____

_____

_____

_____

_____

What are you doing to express your feelings of relief and release?

_____

_____

_____

_____

_____

_____

_____

_____

_____

_____

_____

_____

OTHER FEELINGS

Are you having other feelings that haven't been covered in this discussion? Please take a few minutes to explain them here.

_____

_____

_____

_____

_____

_____

_____

_____

_____

_____

_____

_____

_____

_____

_____

_____

_____

_____

_____

_____

_____

_____

_____

_____

_____

_____

_____

_____

FREE WRITE

_____

_____

_____

_____

_____

_____

_____

_____

_____

_____

_____

_____

_____

_____

_____

_____

_____

_____

_____

_____

_____

_____

_____

_____

_____

_____

_____

_____

_____

_____

_____

Touchstone Five

Recognize You Are Not Crazy

In the companion text…

We discussed the common feeling people in grief have that they are going crazy. Many of the thoughts and feelings you will experience in your journey through grief are so different from your everyday reality that you may feel you're going crazy. You're not. You're just grieving. The two can feel remarkably similar sometimes. This chapter also explores a number of typical thoughts and feelings that contribute to the feeling of going crazy in grief.

SUDDEN CHANGES IN MOOD

Have you experienced some rollercoaster mood changes during the grief experience? Explore below.

_____

_____

_____

_____

_____

_____

_____

_____

_____

_____

_____

_____

MEMORY LAPSES AND TIME DISTORTION

Have you experienced some memory lapses and time distortion? Explain below.

_____

_____

_____

_____

_____

_____

_____

_____

_____

_____

_____

_____

POLYPHASIC BEHAVIOR AND THINKING CHALLENGES

Have you experienced polyphasic behavior and thinking challenges? Explain below.

_____

_____

_____

_____

_____

_____

_____

_____

_____

_____

_____

_____

PSYCHIC NUMBING, DISORIENTATION, DISCONNECTION

Have you experienced any psychic numbing, disorientation, and disconnection? Explore below.

_____

_____

_____

_____

_____

_____

_____

_____

_____

_____

_____

SELF-FOCUS OR FEELING SELFISH

Have you experienced being self-focused or feeling selfish?
Explore below.

_____

_____

_____

_____

_____

_____

_____

_____

_____

_____

RETHINKING AND RESTORATIVE RETELLING OF THE STORY

Are you rethinking and/or retelling the story? If some, take some
time to describe it here.

_____

_____

_____

_____

_____

_____

_____

_____

_____

_____

POWERLESSNESS AND HELPLESSNESS

Has this grief experience resulted in you feeling powerless or helpless at times? In what ways?

_____

_____

_____

_____

_____

_____

_____

_____

_____

_____

_____

_____

LOSS OF ENERGY AND LETHARGY OF GRIEF

Have you experienced loss of energy and lethargy? If so, describe below.

_____

_____

_____

_____

_____

_____

_____

_____

_____

_____

_____

A FEELING OF BEFORE THE SUICIDE AND AFTER THE SUICIDE

Have you experienced this "before and after" phenomenon? If so, describe below.

_____

_____

_____

_____

_____

_____

_____

_____

_____

_____

_____

EXPRESSING FEELINGS MORE OPENLY THAN IN THE PAST

Do you find yourself being more expressive of feelings than you have been in the past? If so, describe below.

_____

_____

_____

_____

_____

_____

_____

_____

_____

GRIEF AND LOSS OVERLOAD

Have you had some special needs because of "loss overload"?
Have you experienced a "ripple effect" from this death? If so,
describe below.

_____

_____

_____

_____

_____

_____

_____

_____

_____

_____

_____

_____

GRIEFBURSTS, PANGS, OR SPASMS

Have you had any griefbursts, pangs, or spasms as part of your
grief journey? If yes, give a few examples below.

_____

_____

_____

_____

_____

_____

_____

_____

_____

_____

_____

CRYING AND SOBBING

Do you find yourself expressing your feelings by crying or sobbing. If so, how do you feel after you are done crying or sobbing? If you are not crying at all, why do you think that is?

_____

_____

_____

_____

_____

_____

_____

_____

_____

_____

_____

_____

BORROWED TEARS

Have you had any experience with borrowed tears? If so, describe what it is like for you.

_____

_____

_____

_____

_____

_____

_____

_____

_____

_____

_____

LINKING OBJECTS AND MEMORABILIA

Do you have some linking objects or memorabilia that connected you to the person who died? If so, what do you have? What have you done—or what do you plan to do—with these items?

_____

_____

_____

_____

_____

_____

_____

_____

_____

_____

_____

_____

CARRIED GRIEF FROM OTHER LOSSES

Do you have any awareness that you might have some carried grief from prior losses? If so, explain. Also, what might you be able to do to give some attention to these prior losses?

_____

_____

_____

_____

_____

_____

_____

_____

_____

_____

SUICIDAL THOUGHTS

Have you considered suicide at any time before or after this death? If yes, write more about your thoughts here. Also see page 76 of this journal for more on suicidal thoughts and determining if you need additional help.

_____

_____

_____

_____

_____

_____

_____

_____

_____

_____

DREAMS OR NIGHTMARES

Have you been having any dreams or disturbing nightmares surrounding this experience? If so, describe them here.

_____

_____

_____

_____

_____

_____

_____

_____

_____

_____

_____

MYSTICAL EXPERIENCES

Have you had any experiences you might describe as "mystical" since the death? If so, describe them here. How did they make you feel?

_____

_____

_____

_____

_____

_____

_____

_____

_____

_____

_____

ANNIVERSARY AND HOLIDAY GRIEF OCCASIONS

In general, what have your birthday, anniversary, and holiday occasions been like for you since this death? Write about your experiences below.

_____

_____

_____

_____

_____

_____

_____

_____

_____

_____

_____

RITUAL-STIMULATED REACTIONS, SEASONAL REACTIONS, MUSIC-STIMULATED REACTIONS, AND AGE-CORRESPONDENCE REACTIONS

Have you experienced the re-stimulation of feelings related to these types of reactions? If so, write about your experiences below.

_____

_____

_____

_____

_____

_____

_____

_____

_____

_____

_____

_____

What other experiences have you had, if any, that you might fit into this chapter? Note them below.

_____

_____

_____

_____

_____

_____

_____

_____

_____

_____

_____

_____

Touchstone Six

Understand the Six Needs Of Mourning

In the companion text...

We introduced the six needs of mourning, which are the six central needs that all mourners must meet in order to heal. Unlike the concept of "stages" of grief, the six needs are not orderly or predictable. You will probably jump around in random fashion while working on them, and you will address each need only when you are ready to do so. Your awareness of these needs, however, will give you a participant, action-oriented approach to integrating this loss into your life as opposed to a perception of this grief as something you passively experience.

Mourning Need 1. Accept the Reality of the Death.

Where do you see yourself in accepting the reality of this death?

_____

_____

_____

_____

_____

_____

Do you think time is playing a part in where you are with this need? If so, how?

_____

_____

_____

_____

_____

_____

Do you understand and allow yourself the need to at times push some of the reality away? If so, how?

_____

_____

_____

_____

_____

_____

What can you do to continue to work on this need?

_____

_____

_____

Mourning Need 2. Let Yourself Feel the Pain of the Loss.

Where do you see yourself in allowing yourself to feel the pain of the loss?

_____

_____

_____

Do you think that time is playing a part in where you are with this need? If so, how?

_____

_____

_____

_____

With whom have you shared your feelings of hurt?

_____

_____

_____

_____

_____

Write about what sharing your feelings has been like for you.

_____

_____

_____

What can you do to continue to work on this need?

_____

_____

_____

Need 3. Remember the Person Who Died.

If you have another favorite picture of the person who died, place it here in your journal:

Where do you see yourself in the process of remembering the person who died?

_____

_____

_____

_____

_____

_____

_____

_____

_____

_____

_____

_____

Write out below a funny or meaningful story about the person who died.

_____

_____

_____

_____

_____

_____

_____

_____

_____

_____

_____

_____

_____

_____

What do you miss the very most about the person who died?

_____

_____

_____

_____

_____

_____

What do you miss the least about the person who died?

_____

_____

_____

_____

_____

What other things will you always remember about the person who died?

_____

_____

_____

_____

_____

What would you want others to always remember about the person who died?

_____

_____

_____

_____

_____

Sayings the person who died used to say are...

_____

_____

_____

_____

_____

_____

_____

_____

_____

_____

The most important thing I learned from the person who died was...

_____

_____

_____

_____

_____

_____

_____

_____

_____

_____

_____

_____

_____

In the space below, write a letter to the person who died. Tell him or her what is in our head and on your heart.

Dear _____,

_____

_____

_____

_____

_____

_____

_____

_____

_____

_____

_____

_____

_____

_____

_____

_____

_____

_____

_____

_____

_____

_____

_____

_____

_____

_____

_____

_____

_____

_____

_____

_____

In the space below, imagine the person who died could write a letter back to you. What do you think he or she would want to say to you?

Dear _____,

_____

_____

_____

_____

_____

_____

_____

_____

_____

_____

_____

_____

_____

_____

_____

_____

_____

_____

_____

_____

_____

_____

_____

_____

_____

_____

_____

_____

What can you do to continue to work on this need?

_____

_____

_____

_____

_____

Need 4. Develop a New Self-Identity.

Where do you see yourself in developing a new self-identity?

_____

_____

_____

_____

_____

What roles did the person who died play in your life?

_____

_____

_____

_____

_____

What identity changes have you experienced as a result of this death?

_____

_____

_____

_____

_____

How do you see people treating you differently as a result of
your changed identity?

_____

_____

_____

_____

_____

_____

_____

_____

_____

Which, if any, positive changes in your self-identity have you
noticed since the death?

_____

_____

_____

_____

_____

_____

_____

_____

_____

What can you do to continue to work on this need?

_____

_____

_____

_____

_____

_____

Need 5. Search for Meaning

Where do you see yourself in your search for meaning?

_____

_____

_____

_____

_____

_____

_____

_____

_____

_____

_____

_____

_____

Do you have any "why?" or "how?" questions right now? If so, what are they?

_____

_____

_____

_____

_____

_____

_____

_____

_____

_____

_____

_____

_____

Are you wrestling with your faith right now? Explain.

_____

_____

_____

_____

_____

_____

_____

_____

_____

_____

_____

_____

_____

What can you do to continue to work on this need?

_____

_____

_____

_____

_____

_____

_____

_____

_____

_____

_____

_____

_____

Studies have shown that prayer can help people heal. If you believe in a higher power, the space below is a safe place for you to write out a prayer.

You might pray about the person who died or about your questions about life and death. You might pray for help in dealing with the pain you feel. You might pray for others affected by this death. Pray for anything that is on your grieving heart.

Dear God,

_____

_____

_____

_____

_____

_____

_____

_____

_____

_____

_____

_____

_____

_____

_____

_____

_____

_____

_____

_____

_____

_____

_____

_____

Need 6. Let Others Help You—Now and Always.

Where do you see yourself in letting others help you—now and always?

_____

_____

_____

_____

_____

_____

_____

_____

_____

_____

_____

_____

Whom do you turn to for help?

_____

_____

_____

_____

_____

_____

_____

_____

_____

_____

_____

_____

_____

_____

What do these people do that lets you know they are there to
support you?

_____

_____

_____

_____

_____

_____

_____

_____

_____

_____

_____

How are you doing at accepting support from people who try to
give it?

_____

_____

_____

_____

_____

_____

_____

_____

_____

_____

_____

_____

_____

_____

Are you getting support from others who have experienced the suicide death of someone loved? Please explain.

_____

_____

_____

_____

_____

_____

_____

_____

_____

_____

What can you do to continue to work on this need?

_____

_____

_____

_____

_____

_____

_____

_____

_____

_____

_____

_____

_____

FREE WRITE

Touchstone Seven

Nurture Yourself

In the companion text…

We reminded ourselves of the need to be self-nurturing in grief. Remember—self-care fortifies you for your long and challenging grief journey. In nurturing ourselves, in allowing ourselves the time and loving attention we need to journey safely and deeply through grief, we find meaning in our continued living. We then explored the five realms in which it is critical to nurture ourselves: physical; emotional; cognitive; social; and spiritual.

NURTURING YOURSELF: THE PHYSICAL REALM

Is your body letting you know that it feels distressed right now? If so, how?

_____

_____

_____

_____

_____

_____

_____

_____

_____

How are you sleeping?

_____

_____

_____

_____

_____

_____

_____

_____

How are you eating?

_____

_____

_____

_____

_____

_____

_____

_____

Of the guidelines outlined in Caring for Your Physical Self, which do you feel you are following right now? List them.

_____

_____

_____

_____

_____

_____

_____

_____

_____

_____

_____

_____

NURTURING YOURSELF: THE EMOTIONAL REALM

What have you been doing to acknowledge and express your feelings?

_____

_____

_____

_____

_____

_____

_____

_____

_____

_____

_____

_____

_____

Have you been journaling, either in this journal or in a different journal? If so, write about what that has been like for you.

_____

_____

_____

_____

_____

_____

_____

_____

What kinds of music touch your heart and your soul? List your favorite artists and types of music here. How does music help you in terms of accessing your feelings?

_____

_____

_____

_____

_____

_____

_____

Make a list of everyday activities that give you pleasure. Pick something from this list each day and do it.

_____

_____

_____

_____

_____

_____

_____

_____

NURTURING YOURSELF: THE COGNITIVE REALM

Have your short-term memory and ability to concentrate been affected by this death. If so, how?

_____

_____

_____

_____

_____

_____

_____

_____

_____

Are you making an effort to not make too many changes too quickly right now? Are there some big decisions you have simply had to make? Write about this below.

_____

_____

_____

_____

_____

_____

_____

_____

_____

_____

_____

_____

115

Have you made some efforts to simplify your life right now? If so, what have you done?

_____

_____

_____

_____

_____

_____

_____

_____

_____

Have you been making daily to-do lists? If so, how is that working for you?

_____

_____

_____

_____

_____

_____

_____

_____

Have you been able to say no and set limits where appropriate? Write about this below.

_____

_____

_____

_____

_____

_____

Have you been practicing patience and being gentle with yourself?

_____

_____

_____

_____

_____

_____

_____

_____

_____

_____

As you explore the list of additional self-care guidelines for caring for your cognitive self, what other things have you been doing? (For example, taking time off work.)

_____

_____

_____

_____

_____

_____

_____

_____

_____

_____

_____

_____

NURTURING YOURSELF: THE SOCIAL REALM

How are you making an effort to stay connected to your family, friends, and community during this time?

_____

_____

_____

_____

_____

_____

_____

_____

_____

_____

_____

_____

Have your friendships changed during this time? If yes, explain. If not, write about why you think your friendships have not changed.

_____

_____

_____

_____

_____

_____

_____

_____

_____

_____

_____

_____

Who are the selected family members you can turn to during this time? Name them and explain why you can turn to them.

_____

_____

_____

_____

_____

_____

_____

_____

_____

_____

_____

_____

_____

_____

Have you reached out to a counselor or participated in a support group at this time? If so, describe what you have done.

_____

_____

_____

_____

_____

_____

_____

_____

_____

_____

_____

_____

Have you scheduled something that gives you pleasure each day? If so, what kinds of things have you done?

_____

_____

_____

_____

_____

_____

_____

_____

_____

_____

_____

_____

_____

_____

Have you done anything to brighten up your living space? If so, what have you done? If not, what could you plan to do?

_____

_____

_____

_____

_____

_____

_____

_____

_____

_____

_____

NURTURING YOURSELF: THE SPIRITUAL REALM

How do you nurture your spirit?

_____
_____
_____
_____
_____
_____
_____
_____
_____
_____
_____
_____

Do you express your faith/spirituality in a body of community?
If so, describe what it is like for you and how it helps you.

_____
_____
_____
_____
_____
_____
_____
_____
_____
_____
_____
_____
_____
_____
_____

Do you have a sacred space of sanctuary? If so, describe it. If not, is there any possibility you could create one? Where and how?

_____

_____

_____

_____

_____

_____

_____

_____

_____

_____

_____

Do you pray? What do you pray for? Describe your prayer practices.

_____

_____

_____

_____

_____

_____

_____

_____

_____

_____

_____

_____

_____

What do you feel gratitude for in your life right now?

_____

_____

_____

_____

_____

_____

_____

_____

_____

_____

As you explore the list of additional self-care guidelines for caring for your spiritual self, what other things might you consider making use of? For example, create a sacred space or sanctuary, celebrate a sunrise, sigh, and spend time in thin places.

_____

_____

_____

_____

_____

_____

_____

_____

_____

_____

_____

_____

FREE WRITE

Touchstone Eight
Reach Out for Help

In the companion text…

We emphasized that healing in grief requires the support and understanding of those around you as you embrace the pain of your loss. You cannot make this journey alone. We also discussed where you can turn for help and how to tell if you need professional help. Finding and working with a grief counselor was explored, as was finding and working with a grief support group.

FELLOW SURVIVORS AND SELECTED FRIENDS AND FAMILY

Note the fellow survivors and family and friends you have turned to at this time. Describe the ways in which they have been helpful to you.

_____

_____

_____

_____

_____

_____

_____

_____

_____

_____

_____

_____

SUPPORT GROUPS

Have you made use of a support group as part of your efforts to help yourself? If so, describe what this experience is like for you.

_____

_____

_____

_____

_____

_____

_____

_____

_____

_____

_____

"HEALTHY" SUPPORT GROUP

If you are making use of a support group, review the signs of a healthy group on page 183. Does your group have these signs?

_____

_____

_____

_____

_____

_____

_____

_____

_____

_____

_____

_____

YOUR RELIGIOUS OR SPIRITUAL COMMUNITY

Have you turned to a religious or spiritual community for support? If so, what has that been like for you?

_____

_____

_____

_____

_____

_____

_____

_____

_____

_____

_____

_____

DR. WOLFELT'S "RULE OF THIRDS"

The rule of thirds says that when you're in grief, you'll typically find that about one-third of the people in your life will be a help to you, one-third will neither help nor harm you, and one-third will be a hindrance to your healing. Below, identify the one-third you believe are helpful to you in your journey through grief.

_____

_____

_____

_____

_____

_____

_____

_____

_____

SAFE PEOPLE: FUNDAMENTAL HELPING ROLES

You learned that "safe people" help you: 1. Feel companioned during your journey; 2. Encounter your feelings related to suicide; 3. Embrace hope. Name the people around you who are able to provide these three helping roles to you.

_____

_____

_____

_____

_____

_____

_____

_____

_____

_____

A PROFESSIONAL COUNSELOR OR CAREGIVER

If you have looked into or are seeing a professional counselor or caregiver, write down the name and contact information right here.

_____

_____

_____

_____

If you are seeing a counselor, what is that experience like for you?

_____

_____

_____

_____

_____

_____

_____

_____

_____

_____

_____

_____

_____

_____

_____

_____

_____

_____

HOW DO I KNOW IF I NEED PROFESSIONAL HELP?

Review the "Red Flags" noted on p. 189. Note any that you are experiencing below. If you have some of these "Red Flags," do remember it is a sign of strength to reach out and find a professional caregiver to help support you at this time.

_____

_____

_____

_____

_____

_____

_____

_____

_____

MEDICATING YOURSELF WITH DRUGS, ALCOHOL, OR OTHER SELF-DESTRUCTIVE BEHAVIORS

Note below any drugs (prescribed and non-prescribed), alcohol, or any behavior you see in yourself that might be hindering you more than helping you. Of course, do not stop taking prescribed medications that you may be using very appropriately. If you see self-destructive use of drugs, alcohol, or behaviors that are harming you more than helping you, get professional help immediately!

_____

_____

_____

_____

_____

_____

_____

_____

FRAMEWORK FOR CONSIDERATION OF GETTING PROFESSIONAL SUPPORT AND COUNSELING

Note below any of the patterns outlined that you see in yourself (postponing, displacing, replacing, minimizing, somaticizing). If you do see any of these in yourself, I encourage you to get professional help immediately.

_____

_____

_____

_____

_____

_____

_____

_____

_____

_____

_____

_____

_____

_____

_____

_____

_____

_____

_____

_____

_____

_____

_____

_____

_____

_____

_____

Free Write

_____
_____
_____
_____
_____
_____
_____
_____
_____
_____
_____
_____
_____
_____
_____
_____
_____
_____
_____
_____
_____
_____
_____
_____
_____
_____
_____
_____
_____
_____
_____
_____

Touchstone Nine

Seek Reconciliation, Not Resolution

In the companion text...

We defined what it means to reconcile your grief instead of recovering from it or resolving it. We explained that as the experience of reconciliation unfolds, you will recognize that life is and will continue to be different without the presence of the person who died. Yet, you will move forward in life with a renewed sense of energy and confidence, an ability to fully acknowledge the reality of the death, and a capacity to become re-involved in the activities of living. We also listed a number of "signs" that reconciliation is taking place in your journey. Finally, we explored the role of continued hope, trust, and faith in the experience of reconciliation.

In the space below, take the opportunity to write out where you see yourself in your own unique healing process. As you have learned about the concept of *reconciliation*, what thoughts and feelings came to mind? Be compassionate with yourself if you are not as far along in your healing as you (or others) would like. After all, through reading *Understanding Your Suicide Grief* and completing this journal, you have certainly created some divine momentum in your healing.

_____

_____

_____

_____

_____

_____

_____

_____

_____

_____

_____

_____

_____

_____

_____

_____

_____

_____

_____

_____

_____

_____

_____

SIGNS OF RECONCILIATION

Which, if any, of the listed signs of reconciliation are you seeing in yourself right now? Note them here.

_____

_____

_____

_____

_____

_____

_____

_____

_____

_____

_____

In the space below, write out what you are doing or have done to help yourself move toward reconciliation.

_____

_____

_____

_____

_____

_____

_____

_____

_____

_____

_____

_____

_____

_____

HOPE FOR YOUR HEALING

Do you have hope for your healing? Explain.

_____

_____

_____

_____

_____

_____

_____

_____

_____

_____

_____

_____

Does your faith sustain you in your journey to reconciliation in grief? Explain.

_____

_____

_____

_____

_____

_____

_____

_____

_____

_____

_____

_____

_____

_____

_____

Do you believe that life continues after death? Explain how this affects your journey to reconciliation in grief.

_____

_____

_____

_____

_____

_____

_____

_____

_____

_____

_____

_____

_____

_____

_____

_____

_____

_____

_____

_____

_____

_____

_____

_____

_____

_____

_____

_____

_____

FREE WRITE

_____

_____

_____

_____

_____

_____

_____

_____

_____

_____

_____

_____

_____

_____

_____

_____

_____

_____

_____

_____

_____

_____

_____

_____

_____

_____

_____

_____

_____

_____

_____

Touchstone Ten

Appreciate Your Transformation

In this chapter in the companion text...

We affirmed that the journey through grief is life-changing, and that when you leave the wilderness of your grief, you are simply not the same person as you were when you entered the wilderness. We also recognized that the transformation you see in yourself—and the personal growth you are experiencing as a result of the death—are not changes you would masochistically seek out. The fact that you are indeed transformed does not mean you are grateful the person died. Still, we explored the various ways in which people grow through grief. We suggested that you have to live not only for yourself, but also for the precious person in your life who has died. We also asked you to consider how you can most authentically live your transformed life from here forward.

APPRECIATE YOUR TRANSFORMATION

You learned that transformation means "an entire change in form." Note below one way in which you have been changed by this death.

_____

_____

_____

_____

_____

_____

_____

_____

_____

_____

_____

_____

GROWTH MEANS CHANGE

Note one or two additional ways you have been changed (new attitudes, insights, awareness).

_____

_____

_____

_____

_____

_____

_____

_____

_____

_____

_____

GROWTH MEANS A NEW INNER BALANCE WITH NO END POINTS

Have you discovered you are in the process of finding a new "inner balance" or a "new normal"? Describe where you see yourself in this process.

_____

_____

_____

_____

_____

_____

_____

_____

_____

GROWTH MEANS EXPLORING YOUR ASSUMPTIONS ABOUT LIFE

Have you noticed that some of your assumptions, values, and priorities have changed since the death? If so, note them below.

_____

_____

_____

_____

_____

_____

_____

_____

_____

_____

_____

GROWTH MEANS UTILIZING YOUR POTENTIAL

How are you making use of your potential?

_____
_____
_____
_____
_____
_____
_____
_____
_____
_____
_____
_____

YOUR RESPONSIBILITY TO LIVE

Do you believe you have a responsibility to live in part on the behalf of the person who died? If yes, why? If no, why not?

_____
_____
_____
_____
_____
_____
_____
_____
_____
_____
_____
_____

NOURISHING YOUR TRANSFORMED SOUL

How do you nourish your transformed soul? List the ways here.

_____

_____

_____

_____

_____

_____

_____

_____

_____

_____

How will you most authentically live your transformed life?

_____

_____

_____

_____

_____

_____

_____

_____

_____

_____

_____

_____

_____

_____

_____

FREE WRITE

Continuing Your Journey

In the months and years to come, I invite you to revisit this book and reflect on the ongoing and ever-changing nature of your journey through grief. How is your grief changing? How do you know you are experiencing reconciliation in your grief? In what ways do you see yourself continuing to transform? Please take a moment now and then to jot down updates in the blank pages that follow. Shalom.

To contact Dr. Wolfelt and for information on his books and workshops, please write, call, or e-mail:

Alan Wolfelt
Center for Loss and Life Transition
3735 Broken Bow Road
Fort Collins, CO 80526
970-226-6050
www.centerforloss.com
DrWolfelt@centerforloss.com

Understanding Your Suicide Grief

When someone loved takes his or her own life, the naturally complex and painful grief that follows is typically overwhelming. The circumstances of the death were traumatic, and the resulting grief for survivors is also traumatic. This compassionate resource explores the unique responses inherent to suicide grief.

Using the metaphor of the wilderness, Dr. Wolfelt introduces ten Touchstones that will assist the survivor in what is often a complicated grief journey. Learning to identify and rely on the Touchstones helps those touched by suicide find their way to hope and healing.

ISBN 978-1-879651-58-6 • 194 pages • softcover • $14.95

The Understanding Your Suicide Grief

Support Group Guide

Meeting Plans for Facilitators

This book is for those who want to facilitate an effective suicide grief support group. It includes 12 meeting plans that interface with Understanding Your Suicide Grief and its companion journal.

ISBN 978-1-879651-60-9 • 44 pages • softcover • $12.95

The Wilderness of Suicide Grief

Finding Your Way

A beautiful, hardcover gift book version of
Understanding Your Suicide Grief

This excerpted version of *Understanding Your Suicide Grief* makes an excellent gift for anyone grieving the suicide death of someone loved. This is an ideal book for the bedside or coffee table. Pick it up before bed and read just a few pages. You'll be carried off to sleep by its gentle, affirming messages of hope and healing.

ISBN 978-1-879651-68-5 • hardcover • 128 pages • $15.95

Living in the Shadow of the Ghosts of Grief
Step into the Light

Reconcile old losses and open the door to infinite joy and love

Are you depressed? Anxious? Angry? Do you have trouble with trust and intimacy? Do you feel a lack of meaning and purpose in your life? You may well be *Living in the Shadow of the Ghosts of Grief.*

When you suffer a loss of any kind—whether through abuse, divorce, job loss, the death of someone loved or other transitions, you naturally grieve inside. To heal your grief, you must express it. That is, you must mourn your grief. If you don't, you will carry your grief into your future, and it will undermine your happiness for the rest of your life.

This compassionate guide will help you learn to identify and mourn your carried grief so you can go on to live the joyful, whole life you deserve.

ISBN 978-1-879651-51-7 • 160 pages • softcover • $13.95